The Oldest Gospel

THE OLDEST GOSPEL

A MISSING LINK IN NEW TESTAMENT SCHOLARSHIP

Newly reconstructed and translated by
Matthias Klinghardt

Quiet Waters Publications
2023

Second edition (revised and enlarged) 2023

Quiet Waters Publications
Springfield, Missouri
www.quietwaterspub.com

Cover design by Sam Trobisch
Final editing by Kai Trobisch

ISBN
978-1-931475-82-2 (hard cover)
978-1-931475-83-9 (paperback)
978-1-931475-84-6 (e-book)

FROM THE PUBLISHER

Few readers will be familiar with the following gospel, which claims to be older than any other book about Jesus. It is attested as early as the second century and was first presented to the public as part of a collection that also contained ten letters of Paul. Its title was simply *Gospel*, and it carried no information about its author. For readers of the collection, Paul endorsed this book with the words: *"If anyone proclaims to you a gospel contrary to what you received, let that one be accursed!"* (Galatians 1:9).

Throughout the centuries, numerous attempts at reconstructing its text were undertaken, but few with the painstakingly detailed effort of Matthias Klinghardt, Professor of New Testament at the University of Dresden, Germany. He critically assessed the quotes, evaluated textual variants, and produced a critical edition of the Greek text. His translation is reprinted here with the permission of the publisher to benefit scholars and students who don't have access to the scholarly tome.[1]

---

[1] Matthias Klinghardt. The Oldest Gospel and the Formation of the Canonical Gospels: Part I: Inquiry. Part II: Reconstruction - Translation - Variants. Vol. 41. Peeters Publishers, 2021. An electronic version is available through JSTOR: https://doi.org/

The critical feedback to the first English version of this reader (2018) led to numerous improvements in this second edition. Specifically, the text now lists chapter and verse numbers and the traditional titles of pericopes to facilitate quotations. For a quick orientation, Matthias Klinghardt added a brief introduction and a table comparing the structure and content of *Gospel (*Evangelium)* with *Gospel according to Luke.*

10.2307/j.ctv1q26qbc. We want to thank Peeters Publishers for the permission to reprint the English translation (p. 1291-1332). The reconstruction assessments are discussed in detail p. 503-1289. The revised German edition (Matthias Klinghardt. Das älteste Evangelium und die Entstehung der kanonischen Evangelien. Tübingen: Francke, 2020, 2nd edition) was translated by Stephen Trobisch.

INTRODUCTION

Origin of *Evangelium*²

Authors of the emerging Catholic Christian movement testify to the existence of this gospel book as early as the second century. However, they did not consider it the oldest gospel, but the late work of a heretic who had published the gospel as part of a collection which also contained ten letters of the Apostle Paul and competed with the canonical New Testament. They identified this heretic as Marcion of Sinope. The text of *Evangelium* is about a third shorter than *Gospel according to Luke*.

The question, therefore, arises: Has *Evangelium* shortened *Gospel according to Luke*, or is *Gospel according to Luke* an enlarged edition of *Evangelium*? Tertullian, who wrote a five-volume work against Marcion, accused him of having "gnawed at the Gospel of Luke like a rat." Marcion, however, insisted that his opponents had expanded *Evangelium*.³

---

2   The asterisk "*" indicates that the text is not directly attested in manuscripts but is reconstructed based on secondary witnesses. "*Evangelium*," the Latin translation of the title "Gospel" is used rather than the original Greek title εὐαγγέλιον, following a long-standing practice of Classical studies to use Latin titles for ancient writings irrespective of their language.

3   Tertullian, *Adversus Marcionem* 1:1:5; 4:4:4.

That Marcion used *Evangelium* does not necessarily prove that he was also its author. Some sources from the 2nd and 3rd centuries claim that "all heretics" used a version of Luke's gospel that was not identical to *Gospel according to Luke*.[4] Celsus, a secular philosopher, who died around 180 CE, states that some Christians changed the oldest gospel three, four, and more times "to deny critical objections" (Origenes, *Contra Celsum* 2:27).

The information that groups outside of the Marcionite movement also used *Evangelium* suggests the book was already in circulation when Marcion encountered it and that Marcion is not its author. Therefore, *Gospel according to Luke* is best understood as an expanded edition of *Evangelium*.

Reconstructing *Evangelium*

Unfortunately, no manuscript of *Evangelium* has so far been discovered. The conflicting text of *Gospel according to Luke* and *Evangelium*, however, encouraged publications in which the promoters of the New Testament sought to prove the inadequacy of the "Marcionite" edition. And as they did so, they quoted it extensively. These refutations are the essential source for reconstructing the text of *Evangelium*.

---

[4]   Cf. Irenaeus, *Adversus Haereses* 3:15:1f; Origenes, *In Lucam homiliae* 16:5; 20:2.

Three stand out among the dozen patristic witnesses because of their detailed treatment of *Evangelium*.[5]

The crucial source is Tertullian from North Africa. At the turn of the 3rd century, he wrote a five-volume refutation of Marcion, of which the third edition survived, dating to 207 CE. The extensive fourth volume discusses *Evangelium* and provides most of the surviving quotations and descriptions.

In the 370s CE, Epiphanius, Bishop of Konstantia (Salamis) in Cyprus, wrote an extensive refutation of 80 heresies. In Book 42, Epiphanius compiled a list of 77 quotations from *Evangelium*, which he used to refute the Marcionite "heresy."

During the 4th century, a fictional dialogue appeared under the pen name of Adamantius. The orthodox protagonist Adamantius talks to representatives of the Marcionites and other "heretical" groups. In the context of the conversation, the Marcionites insist that Adamantius only use *Evangelium* and not quote from his New Testament. These quotations would have lost their argumentative power if they were not accurate.

---

[5] Other Patristic authors providing information on the text of *Evangelium* are Clement of Alexandria; Ephraem Syrus (and PsEphraem); Eznik of Kołb; Irenaeus; Jerome; Hippolytus; Origen; Philastrius; and PsTertullian.

Therefore, they provide a most valuable source for reconstructing *Evangelium.

Methodology

Unfortunately, compiling the individual testimonies leaves the researcher with an impressive number of fragments but does not produce a coherent text.

Comparing *Evangelium with Gospel according to Luke shows that the passages not found in *Evangelium can easily be understood as later additions. The assumption that *Evangelium was created by redacting Gospel according to Luke causes contradictions. If, for example, "Marcion" wanted to cut out all positive references to Jewish scriptures, why did he not always do it? Isn't it more probable that those who produced the New Testament, which consistently portrays Jesus as fulfilling scriptural prophecies, would add references to Old Testament passages to stress their theological interests? From this perspective, the editorial direction runs from *Evangelium to Gospel according to Luke. And thus, the anonymous *Evangelium is older.[6]

Assuming that Gospel according to Luke is an expanded version of *Evangelium, it is likely that the uncontested passages in the text belong to Gospel according to Luke. This assumption is supported by the

---

[6] For an exhaustive discussion of this argument see Klinghardt, *The Oldest Gospel*, 115-183.

observation that patristic sources frequently employ a specific keyword to refer to the lengthier omissions they encountered in *Evangelium,* which aligns with the content found in the Lukan text.

As time passed, quotations from *Evangelium* conflated with *Gospel according to Luke.* Based on this observation, in cases where the sources provide variants to the text of *Evangelium,* the wording furthest from the canonical text most likely represents the oldest text of *Evangelium.*

These considerations are not undisputed, and other methodological assumptions will result in different reconstructions.[7]

Matthias Klinghardt, Dresden, January 2023

---

[7] Reconstructions based on differing methodologies are, for example: Dieter T. Roth, *The Text of Marcion's Gospel* (NTTSD 49), Leiden – London: Brill, 2015; Jason D. BeDuhn, *The First New Testament. Marcion's Scriptural Canon,* Salem (OR): Polebridge, 2013. Cf. the discussion in Klinghardt, *Oldest Gospel,* 409-441.

THE CONTENTS OF *EVANGELIUM

This table of contents is intended to show the major differences between *Evangelium and Gospel according to Luke. Passages in square brackets indicate Lukan additions to *Evangelium, discerning between clearly documented additions (⟦ ⟧) and probable ones ([ ]).

*Title

⟦1,1-2,52   Prologue. Stories of John the Baptist's and Jesus' Birth⟧

*3,1a   Timeline

4,31-37   The Exorcism in the Synagogue of Capharnaum

⟦3,1b-4,13   John the Baptist. Baptism. Genealogy. Temptation⟧

[4,14f   Summary of the Healings in Galilee]

*4,16-30   Rejection at Nazara

[4,38f   Healing Peter's Mother-in-Law]

*4,40-41   Exorcisms in the Evening. Messiah Declaration by the Demons

*4,42-43   Jesus' Retreat into Solitude and Reference to His Ministry

*4,44   Summary. Proclaiming in the Synagogues of Galilee

*5,1-11   Miraculous Catch of Fish. Calling of Peter and the Sons of Zebedee

*5,12-16   Healing the Leper. [Jesus' Retreat]

*5,17-26   Healing the Paralytic

*5,27-32   Calling of Levi. Meal with Tax Collectors

*5,33-39   Question about Fasting

*6,1-5   Plucking Grain on the Sabbath. {The Sabbath Worker}

*6,6-11   Healing the Withered Hand

*6,12-16   The Selection of the Twelve

*6,17-19   The Descent from the Mountain. The Rush of the Crowd

*6,20-26   Sermon on the Plain I: Beatitudes and Woes

*6,27-38   Sermon on the Plain II: {Talion.} Love for Enemies. Charging no Interest. Compassion
*6,39-49   Sermon on the Plain III: Admonitions and Metaphors. [The Wise and the Foolish Builders]
*7,1-10   The Centurion in Capharnaum and His Slave
*7,11-17   Raising the Young Man at Nain
*7,17-23   John the Baptist Taking Offense and His Request
*7,24-28   The Instruction about John
[7,29-35   The Children of Wisdom]
*7,36-50   Anointment by the Sinful Woman
*8,1-3   Support by Prestigious Women
*8,4-18   Parable of the Sower. Purpose of Parables and Explanation
*8,19-21   The Mother of Jesus and His Brothers
*8,22-25   Calming the Storm on the Lake
*8,26-39   Casting out the Demon Legion
*8,40-56   The Daughter of Jairus. The Hemorrhaging Woman
*9,1-6   The Mission of the Twelve
*9,7-9   Herod's Judgment of Jesus and John
*9,10-17   The Return of the Apostles. Feeding the Five Thousand
*9,18-22   Peter's Avowal. First Prediction of Jesus' Death
*9,23-27   Demands of Discipleship
*9,28-36   Jesus' Transfiguration
*9,37-45   Reproaching the Unbelieving Generation. Exorcism of the Epileptic Boy. Second Prediction of Jesus' Death
*9,45-50   Status Dispute among the Disciples. The Unknown Exorcist
*9,51-56   The Mission in Samaria
*9,57-62   Sayings about Discipleship
*10,1-16   Sending out the Seventy-Two Apostles
*10,17-24 The Return of the Seventy-Two. Jesus Giving Thanks
*10,25-37 Question about the Conditions of Life [The Parable of the Good Samaritan]
*10,38-42 Mary and Martha
*11,1-4   The Lord's Prayer

*11,5-13   Instruction about Praying
*11,14-32   Exorcizing a Mute Demon. The Beelzebul Accusation.
            The Return of the Demons. Blessing Those Who Hear
            the Word of God. The Refusal of a Sign.
            ⟦Sign of Jonah⟧
*11,33-36   The Eye as a Beacon of the Body
*11,37-48   Speech to the Pharisees I: Purity. Paying the Tithe.
            The Murder of Prophets
*11,49-54   Speech to the Pharisees II: ⟦Commissioning and Mur-
            der of Prophets and Apostles.⟧ Conclusion
*12,1-12   Warning against the Hypocrisy of the Pharisees.
            The Appeal of Fearless Acknowledgment
*12,13-21   Warning against Greed. The Rich Farmer
*12,22-34   About Worrying. Striving for the Kingdom of God
*12,35-48   Instruction about Vigilance and Trustworthiness
*12,49-53   Peace and Discord
*12,54-59   Judging this *kairos*. Reconciling with the Adversary
⟦13,1-9   Repentance Request. Parable of the Barren Fig Tree⟧
*13,10-17   Healing a Daughter of Abraham on the Sabbath
*13,18-21   Parables of the Mustard Seed and the Yeast
*13,22-30   The Narrow and the Shut Door.
            ⟦The First and the Last in the Kingdom of God ⟧
⟦13,31-35   Warning against Herod. Lament over Jerusalem⟧
*14,1-6   Healing a Man with Dropsy on a Sabbath
*14,7-24   Admonitions about Invitations to Meals
*14,25-35   Requirements for Being a Disciple
⟦15,1-2   The Pharisees and scribes grumbling about Jesus eat-
            ing with sinners ⟧
*15,3-10   The Parables of the Lost Sheep and the Lost Coin
⟦15,11-32   Parable of the Prodigal Son and His Brother⟧
*16,1-13   The Parable of the Dishonest Manager.
            Being Faithful in a Very Little and in Much
*16,14-18   Against the Pharisees: Greed. The Law and the
            Prophets.
            Divorce and Remarriage
*16,19-31   The Parable of the Poor Lazarus and the Rich Neves

*17,1-10   Speech to the Disciples about Temptation and about the Power of Faith
*17,11-19   Cleansing Ten Lepers
*17,20-21   About the Coming of the Kingdom of God
*17,22-37   About the Coming of the Son of Man
*18,1-8   Parable of the Pleading Widow
*18,9-14   The Parable of the Pharisee and the Tax Collector in the Temple
*18,15-17   Blessing of the Children
*18,18-23   The Question about the Requirements for Eternal Life
*18,24-30   Wealth and Succession
[18,31-34   Third Passion Prediction]
*18,35-43   Healing a Blind Man in Jericho
*19,1-10   The Conversion of Zacchaeus
*19,11-28   The Parable of the Ten Pounds. Entry into Jerusalem
19,29-48   [Finding the Riding Animal.]
            Acclamation at the Mount of Olives.
            [Dominus flevit. Cleansing of the Temple.]
            [Instruction in the Temple. Intention to Kill Jesus.]
*20,1-8   Questioning Jesus' Authority
[20,9-18   Parable of the Wicked Tenants]
*20,19   The Intent to Arrest Jesus
*20,20-26   The Question about Paying Taxes to the Emperor
*20,27-40   The Question about the Resurrection
*20,41-44   The Messiah is David's Lord, Not His Son
*20,45-47   Warning about the Scribes
*21,1-4   The Widow's Offering
*21,5-36   Speech about the End Times
*21,37-38   Concluding Summary: Teaching in Jerusalem
*22,1-6   The Intent to Kill Jesus by the Chief Priests. The Betrayal of Judas
*22,7-13   The Preparation of the Passover Meal
*22,14-23   The Last Supper. Announcing the Betrayal
*22,24-34   Meal Conversations: The Disciples Disputing Status. The Announcement of Peter's Denial
[22,35-38   The Moment of Decision]
*22,39-46   Prayer on the Mount of Olives

*22,47-53   Encounter with the Arrest Squad

*22,54-65   Peter's Denial. Mockery of Jesus by the Guards

*22,66-71   Interrogation before the High Council

*23,1-5   The Trial of Jesus I: Transfer to Pilate.
Interrogation and First Judgment by Pilate

*23,6-12   The Trial of Jesus II: Transfer to Herod. Interrogation.
Mockery

*23,13-25   The Trial of Jesus III: Repeating the Innocence Declaration.
Barabbas. Sentencing

*23,26-32   The Way of the Cross: Simon of Cyrene.
The Women of Jerusalem. Two Criminals

*23,33-49   Crucifixion and Death of Jesus

*23,50-56   Burial of Jesus

*24,1-12   Finding the Empty Tomb. The Angels' Proclamation.
Message to the Disciples

*24,13-35   Appearance to Emmaus/Amaus and Cleopas

*24,36-49   Jesus' Appearance to the Disciples

*24,50-53   Commissioning of the Disciples. The Departure of
Jesus.
[Ascension to Heaven.] The Return to Jerusalem

CRITICAL MARKS

The following critical marks are used:

italics   Obscure attestation or obscure wording; particularly in passages for which no assessment is possible.

{ }   Words or passages of *Evangelium* that were omitted by the Lukan redaction.

↑ ↓   Rearrangements in *Gospel according to Luke* opposed to the text of *Evangelium*.

( )   Added by the translator for clarity.

(D)   (Following chapter and verse numbers) indicates a reading from Codex Bezae (D 05).

Bold headings were not part of the text of *Evangelium*.

TRANSLATION

*Title

Gospel

*3,1a; 4,31–37: The Exorcism in the Synagogue of Capharnaum

^{3,1a} In the 15th year of the reign of Emperor Tiberius, ^{4,31} {Jesus} went down to Capharnaum, a city in Galilee {at the sea in the territory of Zebulon and Naphtali}. And he taught them on the Sabbath days. ³² And all were astounded at his teaching because he spoke with authority. ³³ And in the synagogue was a man who had the spirit of an unclean demon, and he cried out with a loud voice, ³⁴ "What have we to do with you, Jesus of Nazara? Have you come to destroy us? I know who you are, the Holy One of God." ³⁵ And Jesus rebuked him, saying, "Be silent, and come out of him!" And the demon threw him into the center and came out of him screaming, but he did not hurt him. ³⁶ And great amazement came over them all, and they spoke among themselves, saying, "What kind of speech is this? For with authority and power he commands the unclean spirits, so that they come out!" ³⁷ And the report about him spread to every place in the region.

*4,16–30: Rejection at Nazara

^{4,16} But when he came to Nazara, he went into the synagogue on the Sabbath day. ^{22b} And they said, "Is not this Joseph's son?" ²³ And he said to them, "Now you will indubitably

quote this proverb to me, 'Physician, heal yourself! Everything that we have heard happening in Capharnaum, do also here in your hometown'." ²⁴ But he said, "Truly, I say to you: No prophet is accepted in his hometown." ²⁸ Then all in the synagogue were filled with anger, ²⁹ and they got up and thrust him out of the city. And they led him to the slope of the mountain on which their city is built to hurl him down. ³⁰ But he passed right through the midst of them and went away.

*4,40–41: Exorcisms in the Evening. Messiah Declaration by the Demons

(Cf. Matt 4,13) *And he left Nazara and went and lived in Capharnaum by the sea, in the territory of Zebulon and Naphtali.* ^{4,40} As the sun was setting, all brought the sick people with various ailments to him, as many as they had. But he laid his hands on each of them and healed them. ⁴¹ But demons came out of many. They cried out, saying, "You are the Son of God!" And rebuking them, he would not let them speak. For they knew that he was the Christ.

*4,42–44: Jesus' Retreat into Solitude and Reference to His Ministry

^{4,42} But when it was day, he left and went to a desert place. And the crowd was looking for him, and they came to him and they firmly held on to him, so that he would not depart from them. ⁴³ But he said to them, "It is necessary that I proclaim the kingdom of God also in the other cities for that is

why I am sent." ⁴⁴ And he preached in the synagogues of Galilee.

*5,1–11: Miraculous Catch of Fish. Calling of Peter and the Zebedees

^{5,1} But it happened that the crowd pressed upon him and heard the word of God. And when he was standing beside Lake Gennesaret, ² there he saw two boats lying by the lake. But the fishermen had gone out of them and washed their nets. ³ He entered into one of the boats which belonged to Simon and asked him to put out a little way from the shore; he sat down in the boat and taught the crowds. ⁴ But when he had finished speaking, he said to Simon, "Put out into the deep water and let down your nets for a catch!" ⁵ But Simon answered, saying to him, "Teacher, we have toiled all night long but caught nothing. But I will not disobey your word." ⁶ And immediately they threw out their nets and enclosed such an amount of fish that their nets were tearing. ⁷ And they waved to their partners in the other boat to come and to help them. And they came and filled both boats, so that they almost sank. ⁸ But Simon fell down at his feet, saying, "Please! Go away from me, for I am a sinful man, Lord!" ⁹ For amazement had seized him about the catch of fish they had taken. ¹⁰ But his partners were James and John, the sons of Zebedee. But he said to them, "Come on! You are no longer fishermen of fish, for I will make you fishermen of people!" ¹¹ But when they heard that, they left everything on the shore behind and followed him.

*5,12–16: Healing the Leper. Jesus' Retreat

^{5,12} And it happened when he was in one of the cities, and see, there was a leper. But when he saw Jesus, he fell on his face, saying, "Lord, if you will, you are able to make me clean." ¹³ And he stretched out his hand, touched him, and said, "I will. Be clean." And immediately he was cleansed. ¹⁴ And he ordered him to tell no one; but rather, "Go, show yourself to the priest, and offer the gift which Moses commanded, so that this bears witness to you."

{^{14 (D)} But he went away and began to proclaim and to spread the word, so that he no longer could publicly enter into a city but was outside in deserted places. And they came to him, and he went again to Capharnaum.}

*5,17–26: Healing the Paralytic

^{5,17} And it happened on a day when he taught that the Pharisees *and scribes* came together. They had come together from every village of Galilee and Judea, so that they would be healed. ¹⁸ And see, men came carrying on a stretcher a man who was paralyzed, and they were trying to bring him inside and set him before him. ¹⁹ But finding no way to bring him inside because of the crowd, they climbed up on the roof, removed the tiles where he was, and let the stretcher with the paralytic down before Jesus. ²⁰ And seeing their faith, he says to the paralytic, "Man, your sins are forgiven you." ²¹ And the scribes and Pharisees began to contemplate {in their hearts,} saying, "What blasphemies does this one speak? Who forgives sins but God alone?" ²² But when Jesus perceived their thoughts, he answered and said to

them, "What evil do you contemplate in your hearts? [23] Which is easier, to say 'Your sins are forgiven you', or to say 'Stand up and walk around'? [24] But so you may see that the Son of Man has authority to forgive sins on earth", he says to the paralytic, "Stand up and take your stretcher and go home." [25] And immediately he stood up before all eyes, took his stretcher, and went home glorifying God. [26b] And they were filled with fear, saying, "Today we have seen incredible things."

*5,27–32: Calling of Levi. Meal with Tax Collectors

5,27 (D) And when he returned again to the sea and a crowd followed him, he taught. And in passing, he saw Levi, son of Alphaeus, sitting at the tax booth, and he says to him, "Follow me!" [28] And he left everything, got up, and followed him. [29] And Levi gave a large dinner for him in his house. And a large crowd of tax collectors and others was there lying at the table with them. [30] And the Pharisees and their scribes grumbled at his disciples and said, "Why do you eat and drink with the tax collectors?" [31] And Jesus answered, saying to them, "Not those who are healthy need a physician, but those who are not well. [32] I have not come to call the righteous."

*5,33–39: Question about Fasting

5,33 And they said to him, "Why do the disciples of John and the disciples of the Pharisees fast steadily and carry out prayers, but yours eat and drink?" [34] Jesus said to them, "Can the wedding guests possibly fast as long as the bridegroom is with them? [35] But days will come, and when the bridegroom is taken away from them, then they will fast in those days.

[37] "New wine is not poured into old wineskins. But if so, the new wine will burst the skins, then the wine is lost and also the skins. [38] Instead, new wine is poured into new wineskins. And both remain preserved.

↑[36b] "And no one sews a piece of unshrunk cloth onto an old cloak. But if so, it all tears, and it will be of no use for the old. For it will result in a larger tear." ↓

*6,1–5: Plucking Grain on the Sabbath. The Sabbath Worker

[6,1] And it happened on the Sabbath that he went through the grain fields, and his disciples even so began to pluck the heads of grain, rubbed them between their hands, and ate them. [2] But the Pharisees said to him, "See, why are your disciples doing what is not allowed on the Sabbath?" [3] But Jesus answered, saying to them, "Have you never read what David has done? [4] He went into the house of God and ate the bread off the altar and gave it also to those who were with him, although it is lawful for no one to eat but the priests alone?"

[4] [(D)] On the same day he saw someone work on the Sabbath and said to him, "Man, if you know what you are doing, you are blessed. But if you do not know it, you are cursed and a trespasser of the law."

*6,6–11: Healing the Withered Hand

6,6 And on the Sabbath he went again into the synagogue in which there was a man whose hand was withered. 7 The Pharisees watched him, whether he would heal on the Sabbath, so that they could accuse him. 8 But when he perceives their thoughts, he says to him who has the withered hand, "Get up and stand at the center." And he got up and stood there. 9 But Jesus said to them, "I ask you, is it lawful to do good things on the Sabbath or not, to redeem a soul or to destroy it?" But they were silent. 10 And he looks at all of them {full of anger}, 10 and he says to the man, "Stretch out your hand." And he stretched it out, and his hand was restored {, exactly as the other}. ↑And he said to them, "The Son of Man is Lord also over the Sabbath." ↓

11 But they were filled with incomprehension, and they deliberated with one another, {how they could destroy him}.

*6,12–16: The Selection of the Twelve

6,12 And he climbed up the mountain and spent the night in prayer. 13 And when day came, he called his disciples. And he selected twelve of them, whom he also called apostles, 14 {as the first} Simon, whom he called Peter, and his brother Andrew; and James and {his brother} John, {whom he called Boanerges, which means, sons of thunder}; and Philip and Bartholomew 15 and Matthew and *Judas* Thomas, {who was called the 'twin'}, and James (son of) Alphaeus and Simon, who was called the Zealot, 16 and Judas (son of) James and Judas from Kerioth, who {also} became the traitor.

*6,17–19a : The Descent from the Mountain. The Rush of the Crowd

6,17 And when he had descended with them, he stopped on a level plain, and also a great crowd of his disciples and a great number of the people from all Judea and from the other shore and from other cities 18 who came to hear him and to be healed of their diseases. And those troubled with unclean spirits were healed, 19 and the entire crowd sought to touch him.

*6,20–26: Sermon on the Plain I: Beatitudes and Woes

6,20 And he lifted up his eyes at his disciples and said,

"Blessed the poor, for theirs is the kingdom of the heavens.

21 "Blessed the hungry, for they will be satisfied.

"Blessed the weeping, for they will laugh.

22 "Blessed will you be when people will hate and vilify you and reject your name as something evil for the sake of the Son of Man. 23 Your fathers have done the same already to the prophets.

24 "But woe to the rich; for you have received your consolation.

25 "Woe to the saturated, for they will go hungry.

"Woe to the laughing, for they will be saddened.

26 "Woe if people speak well of you. That is what your fathers have done also to the false prophets."

*6,27–31.34–38: Sermon on the Plain II: {Talion.} Love for Enemies. Charging no Interest. Compassion

6,27 "{*In the law it is written:* Eye for eye, tooth for tooth.} But to you that listen to me, I say: Love your enemies 28 and pray for those who persecute you.

29 "If anyone strikes you on the {right} cheek, offer to him also the other. And if anyone takes away your coat, give him also your shirt! 30 Give to everyone who asks you! 31 And as you want to be treated by others, so you should do to them.

34 "And if you lend to those from whom you hope to receive, of what kind is your gratitude? 35 But love your enemies and do good things and lend when you can expect nothing in return. Then your reward will be great, and you will be sons of God. For he is kind toward the ungrateful and the wicked.

36 "Be merciful, just as your Father had mercy on you.

37 "And do not judge, so that you will not be judged.

"And do not condemn, so that you will not be condemned.

"Forgive, and you will be forgiven.

38 "Give, and you will be given. A good measure, pressed down and running over, will be placed into your lap! By the measure you will be giving out, you will be measured."

*6,39–46: Sermon on the Plain III: Admonitions and Metaphors

6,39 "Can a blind person possibly guide a blind person? Will not both fall into the pit? 40 The disciple is not above the

22

teacher. *But everyone made complete will be like his teacher.*

⁴¹ "Why do you look at the woodchip in the eye of your brother, but the log in your own eye you do not notice? ⁴² How can you say to your brother, 'Brother, leave me be, I remove the woodchip from your eye!', and see, the log lies in your eye? Hypocrite! First remove the log from your eye, and then see that you remove the woodchip from the eye of your brother.

⁴³ "It is not possible that a good tree bears bad fruit and neither that a bad tree bears good fruit. ⁴⁴ For each tree will be known by its own fruit. For from thistles no figs are gathered, and from a brier no grapes are picked. ⁴⁵ A good person brings forth what is good from the good treasure of his heart, and the bad person what is bad from the bad. For from the overabundance of the heart, his mouth speaks.

⁴⁶ "Why do you cry out, 'Lord, Lord!', and do not do what I say?"

*7,1–10: The Centurion in Capharnaum and His Slave

⁷,¹ And it happened as he had finished speaking these words that he came to Capharnaum. ² The boy of a centurion was ill and close to death; he was dear to him. ³ But when he heard about Jesus, he sent elders of the Jews, asking him whether he may come and save his slave. ⁴ When they came to Jesus, they eagerly appealed to him, saying, "He is worthy that you grant him this. ⁵ For he loves our people and has built the synagogue for us." ⁶ And Jesus went with them. But when he was not far from the house, he sent his friends.

The centurion said to him, "Lord, do not trouble yourself. For I am not worthy that you come under my roof. [7] But speak a word, and my boy will be healed. [8] For I also am a man set under an authority, and I have soldiers under me. And I say to one, 'Go!' and he goes, and to another, 'Come!' then he comes, or to my slave, 'Do this!' then he does it." [9] But when Jesus heard this, he was surprised. And he turned to the crowd that followed him, saying, "Truly, I say to you: With no one have I found faith of such kind in Israel." [10] And the slaves who had been sent returned to the house and found him healthy.

*7,11–16: Raising the Young Man at Nain

[7,11] And on the following day he came to a town called Nain, *and his disciples and a large crowd came with him.* [12] But it happened, as he approached the gate of the town, and see, someone who had died was carried to his grave, the only son of his mother who was a widow. And a large crowd from the town went with her. [13] And when Jesus saw her, he had compassion for her and said to her, "Do not weep!" [14] And he came forward and touched the corpse; but the bearers stood still. And he said, "Young man, young man, I say to you: Rise!" [15] And the dead man sat up and began to speak, and he gave him to his mother. [16] Fear seized them all, and they glorified God, saying, "A great prophet has risen among us, and God has visited his people."

*7,17–23: John the Baptist Taking Offense and His Request

7,17 And this news about him spread throughout Judea, even to John the Baptist. ¹⁸ *When he heard of his deeds, he took offense*. And he summons two of his disciples, ¹⁹ {saying, "Go, say to him,} 'Are you the one who comes, or shall we wait for another?'" ²⁰ But when the men came to him, they said, "John the Baptist has sent us to you, saying, 'Are you the one who comes, or shall we to wait for another?'" ²² And he answered, saying to them, "Go and tell John what your eyes have seen and your ears have heard: the blind see again, the lame walk, the lepers are cleansed and the deaf hear, the dead are raised, the poor are proclaimed good tidings. ²³ And blessed *are you*, if you take no offense at me!"

*7,24–28: The Instruction about John

7,24 When John's messengers had gone, he began to speak to the crowds about John: "What did you go out into the wilderness to behold? Perhaps a reed shaken by the wind? ²⁵ Or what then did you go out to see? Perhaps a man covered in soft robes? See, those who live in festive clothing and in luxury are in the palaces! ²⁶ What then did you go out to see? – Perhaps a prophet? Yes, I say to you, and even more than a prophet! For among those born of women there is no greater prophet than John the Baptist. ²⁷ He is the one about whom it is written: 'See, I am sending my messenger before your face who will prepare the way for you.' ²⁸ But the least in the kingdom is greater than he."

*7,36–50: Anointment by the Sinful Woman

^{7,36} But one of the Pharisees invited him to dine with him. And he went into the Pharisee's house and laid down. ³⁷ And see, a woman, a sinner *in the city*, stood behind him at his feet. She bathed his feet with her tears and salved him with ointment.

³⁹ But when {Simon Peter} saw this, he said to himself, "If this man were a prophet, he would know who and of what kind the woman is who touches him, for she is a sinner." ⁴⁰ And Jesus answered, saying to Peter, "Simon, I have something to say to you." He said, "Teacher, speak." ⁴⁴ And he turned to the woman, saying to Simon, "Do you see this woman? She has washed my feet with her tears, ↑⁴⁶ she has anointed↓ ↑⁴⁵ and kissed me.↓ ⁴⁷ Therefore, I say to you, her many sins are forgiven, for she has loved much."

⁴⁸ But to her he said, "Your sins are forgiven." ⁴⁹ And those lying at the table with him began to say among themselves, "Who is this one who even forgives sins?" ⁵⁰ But he said to the woman, "Your faith has saved you. Go in peace."

*8,2–3: Support by Prestigious Women

^{8,2} And some women were cured of evil spirits and illnesses: Mary, called the Magdalene, from whom seven demons had gone out, ³ and Joanna, the wife of Chuza, a steward of Herod, and Susanna, and many others. They also supported him from their resources.

*8,4–17: Parable of the Sower. Purpose of Parables and Explanation

[8,4] But when a great crowd gathered and people from every town came to him, he spoke to them in a parable like this: [5] "The sower went out to sow his seed. And as he sowed, some fell on the path, and it was crushed, and the birds ate it up. [6] And some fell on rocks, and it grew up and withered because it had no moisture. [7] And some fell among thorns; and as the thorns grew with it, they choked it. [8] And some fell on good and beautiful soil, and when it had grown, it yielded a hundredfold fruit." As he said this, he called out, "Anyone who has ears, listen!"

[9] But his disciples asked him what this parable might be. [10a] But he said, "To you it has been given to know the secrets of the kingdom of God! ↑[18] Pay attention to how you listen! For to him who has, more will be given. But from him who does not have, even what he seems to have will be taken away.↓ [10b] But to others it {will not been given, except} in a parable, so that they, although they see, do not see, and although they listen, do not understand.

[11] "And the parable is this: The seed is the word of God. [12] But the ones on the path are those who have heard; then the devil comes and takes away the word from their hearts, so that they do not believe and are not saved. [13] And the ones on the rock are those who receive the word with joy when they hear it; but these have no root, they believe for a certain time and at the time of the temptation, they fall away. [14] But what fell among the thorns are those who have heard. But through sorrows and riches and pleasures of life

they are choked, so that they do not reach the destination. [15] But that on the good soil, they are the ones who hear the word with a noble heart and adhere to it and bear fruit with patience.

[16] "No one lights a lamp and then hides it. [17] For nothing is hidden that will not be revealed and nothing secret that will not become known and come to light."

*8,20–21: The Mother of Jesus and His Brothers

[8,20] And he was told that his mother and his brothers are standing outside and whishing to see him. [21] But he answered, saying to them: "{Who is} my mother and {who are} my brothers, {if not} those who hear my words {and keep them}?"

*8,22–25: Calming the Storm on the Lake

[8,22] And it happened on one of the days that he stepped into a boat and also his disciples. And he said to them, "Let us go across to the other shore of the lake." And they put out. [23] But while they were sailing he fell asleep. A windstorm swept down on the lake, so that (the boat) filled (with water), and they were in danger. [24] They moved toward him and woke him up, saying, "Teacher, we are going to perish!" But when he had gotten up, he rebuked the wind and the sea. And they calmed down, and a stillness set in. [25] But he said to them, "Where is your faith?" But filled with fear they were amazed, saying to one another, "Who is he who commands even the winds and the sea, so that they obey him?"

*8,26–37: Casting out the Demon Legion

8,26 And they sailed to the country of the Gerasenes which lies across from Galilee. 27 But as he stepped out, he was met on land by a man from the city who had been possessed by demons for a long time. He wore no upper garment and did not live in a house, but in the tombs. 28 When he saw Jesus, he shouted with a loud voice, saying, "What have I to do with you, Jesus, Son of God? I beg you, do not torment me!" 29 For he had commanded the unclean demon, "Come out of this man!" *For it had seized him many times, and he had been bound with chains and fettered at his feet, and because he tore his fetters, he was driven into the desert by the demon.*

30 But Jesus asked him, "What is your name?" And he said, "Legion is my name", for there were many demons. 31 And they begged him not to give them the command of being driven into the abyss. 32 But there was a herd of swine feeding at the hillside. And they begged him for permission to enter the swine; and he permitted them. 33 As the demons drove out of the man, they rushed into the swine, and the herd rushed down the steep bank into the lake and drowned.

34 When the swineherds saw what happened, they fled and told about it in the city and in the hamlets. 35 But when those from the city came near and saw that the possessed man was in his right mind and sitting at the feet of Jesus clothed, they were afraid. 36 And those who had seen how the possessed man was saved told them. 37 But everyone and the country of the Gerasenes begged Jesus to depart

from them, for they were gripped by great fear. But he got in and returned.

*8,40–56: The Daughter of Jairus. The Hemorrhaging Woman

8,40 But it happened when Jesus returned that the crowd welcomed him, for everyone greeted him. 41 And see, there came a man named Jairus, and he was a synagogue leader, and he fell down at the feet of Jesus and begged him to come to his house, 42 for his only daughter at twelve years of age lay dying.

But it happened, as he went to his house, that the crowd almost crushed him. 43 And there was a woman who had been suffering from hemorrhages for twelve years, and not a single person could heal her. 44 She came near and touched his clothes, and immediately her hemorrhage stopped. 45 {When Jesus noticed that power had gone out from him, he asked,} "Who has touched me?" When all denied it, Peter said, "Teacher, the crowd surrounds you and keeps pushing." 46 But Jesus said: "Someone has touched me. I well know that power has gone out from me." 47 When the woman saw that she was not unnoticed, she came forth trembling and fell down at his feet and declared before all the people the reason why she had touched him and how she was immediately healed. 48 But he said to her, "Daughter, your faith has saved you. Go in peace."

49 While he was still speaking, they came from the synagogue leader, saying, "Your daughter is dead. Trouble the teacher no more!" 50 But when Jesus heard that, he replied

to him, "Do not fear, only believe, then she will be saved!" [51] But when he entered the house, he did not permit anyone to enter with him except Peter and John and James and the child's father and the mother. [52] But everyone wept and wailed for her. But he said, "Do not weep, for she has not died, but sleeps." [53] And they laughed at him because they knew that she had died. [54] But he took her by the hand, called out and said, "Get up, child!" [55] And her spirit returned, and she got up at once. And he bade to give her something to eat. [56] And her parents were beside themselves. But he ordered them to say to no one what happened.

*9,1–6: The Mission of the Twelve

[9,1] But he called his twelve disciples together and gave them the power and the authority over all demons, [2] and he sent the disciples out to proclaim the kingdom of God. [3] And he said to them, "Take nothing with you on the journey, neither a staff nor a bag, neither bread nor money, nor (should you) have two undergarments. [4] And when you enter a house, stay there and leave from there. [5] And those who do not receive you, walk away from that town and shake the dust off your feet as a testimony against them!" [6] But they departed and travelled through all towns and villages, proclaiming the Gospel everywhere.

*9,7–9: Herod's Judgment of Jesus and John

[9,7] But when *King* Herod heard about what happened, he became perplexed because some said, "John has been

raised from the dead", [8] and others, "Elijah has appeared", and yet others said, "One of the ancient prophets has arisen". [9] But Herod said, "I beheaded John. Who is this man about whom I hear such things?" *And he sought to meet him.*

*9,10–17: The Return of the Apostles. Feeding the Five Thousand

[9,10] And the apostles returned and told him all they had done. And he welcomed them and went with them alone to a secluded place called Bethsaida. [11] But the crowd became aware of it and followed him. And he received them and spoke to them about the kingdom of God; and he healed all those in need of his care.

[12] But the day began to wear away. And the Twelve approached him, saying to him, "Dismiss the crowd, so that they may go into the surrounding villages and lodge in the farmsteads, for here they are in a secluded place!" [13] But he said to them, "Give them to eat!" But they said, "We only have five loaves of bread and two fish, other than that we leave and then buy food for all these people." [14] For there were about five thousand men. But he said to his disciples, "Make them gather in groups of about fifty each!" [15] And they did so. [16] But he took the five loaves of bread and the two fish, looked up to heaven, prayed and spoke the blessing over them, and gave them to the disciples, so that they hand them out to the crowd. [17] And they ate, and all were satisfied. And what was left over in bits was gathered up: twelve baskets.

*9,18–22: Peter's Avowal. First Prediction of Jesus' Death

18 And it happened, when the disciples were together with him alone, he asked them, saying, "Who do the people take me for, the Son of Man?" 19 And the disciples said, "for John the Baptist, others for Elijah or one of the prophets." 20 But he said to them, "But who do you (take me for)?" But Peter answered, saying, "You are the Christ, *the Son*." 21 But he berated them and demanded to tell this to no one, 22 saying, "It is necessary that the Son of Man suffers much and be killed, but after three days raised again."

*9,23–27: Demands of Discipleship

9,23 But he said to them all, "If someone wants to follow behind me, let him deny himself and then follow me. 24 For he who wants to save his life will lose it. And he who loses his life for my sake will save it. 25 For what is the use if a man gains the whole world but loses himself or suffers harm? 26 He who is ashamed of me *and of those who belong to me*, of him I also will be ashamed. 27 But truly, I say to you: There are some among those standing here who will not taste death before they will see the coming of the Son of Man in his glory."

*9,28–36: Jesus' Transfiguration

9,28 *But it happened about eight days after these sayings that he took Peter and John and James with him and ascended the mountain.* 29 And while he prayed, it happened: the appearance of his face changed, and his clothes became dazzling white. 30 And see, two men spoke with him, Elijah and Moses [31] in glory. [33] Peter said to Jesus, "Teacher, it is good that we are here. And we want to put up three tents here, one for you and for Moses one and for Elijah one" – without knowing what he said. [34] But while he was saying this, a cloud emerged, overshadowing them. But they were frightened when they entered into the cloud. [35] And a voice (came) from the cloud, "This is my Son and my Beloved; listen to him!" [36] And when the voice had faded, Jesus was found alone. And they kept silent and in those days told no one what they had seen.

*9,37–45: Reproaching the Unbelieving Generation. Exorcism of the Epileptic Boy. Second Prediction of Jesus' Death

[9,37] But it happened on the day he came down from the mountain that a great crowd gathered to meet him. [38] And see, a man from the crowd called for help, saying, "Teacher, I beg you, look at my son, for he is my only one." [39] For a spirit seizes him suddenly and snatches him and lets him twitch with foam; almost never does it let go of him and smashes him to pieces. [40] And I have begged your disciples, but they could not cast it out." [41] And he said {to them}: "Faithless generation! How long must I put up with you? Bring your son!" [42] But while he was still bringing him, the demon broke loose and tore at him in convulsions. But Jesus berated the unclean spirit, so that he let go of him, and he gave the boy to his father. [43] And all were beside themselves because of the greatness of God.

But while they all wondered about everything that he had done, he said to his disciples, [44] "Plug these words into your ears: The Son of Man will be delivered into the hands of men." [45] But they did not understand this saying.

*9,45–50: Status Dispute among the Disciples. The Unknown Exorcist

[45b] And they were afraid to ask him about this saying, [46] which of them was the greatest. [47] But Jesus, knowing the thought in their hearts, took a child, placed it by his side, [48] and said, "Whoever accepts this child in my name, accepts me and the one who sent me. For the least among you all is great."

[49] But John answered, saying, "Teacher, we saw someone casting out demons in your name. And we stopped him because he does not follow together with us." [50] But Jesus said to them, "Do not stop him, for he is not against you and not for you. {For there is no one who does a deed of power, except in my name.}"

*9,52–56: The Mission in Samaria

[9,52] And he sent messengers ahead of him. And when they were on their way, they entered a village of the Samaritans to prepare quarters for him. [53] But they did not welcome him. [54] But when his disciples James and John saw that, they said, "Lord, do you want us to say that fire comes down from heaven and consumes them, *as Elijah has done*?" [55] But he turned against them and threatened them. {And he said, "You do not know of what spirit you are. [56] For the

Son of Man has not come to destroy the life of men but to save it."} And they went into another village.

*9,57–62: Sayings about Discipleship

⁵⁷ And it happened as they were going along the road that someone said to him, "I want to follow you wherever you go." ⁵⁸ And Jesus said to him, "The foxes have their holes, and the birds in the sky have their nests where they rest, but the Son of Man has nothing where he lays down his head."

⁵⁹ He said to Philip: "Follow me!" But Philip said, "Permit me that I first go to bury my father." ⁶⁰ But he said to him, "Let the dead bury their dead; but you follow me!"

⁶¹ But another said, "I will follow you, Lord. But first permit me that I say farewell to those in my house." ⁶² But Jesus said to him, "No one who looks back and puts the hand to the plow is fit for the kingdom of God."

*10,1–16: Sending out the Seventy–Two Apostles

But he also appointed seventy-two other apostles next to the Twelve and sent them in pairs *to every city and every place.*

² But he said to them, "The harvest is plentiful, but there are few laborers. Ask the Lord of the harvest to send out laborers into his harvest. ³ Go! See, I send you out like lambs into the midst of wolves. ⁴ Take no purse, no bag, {no staff,} no shoes. And greet no one on the road. ⁵ When you enter a house, say, 'Peace to this house!' ⁶ And if there is a son of peace, your peace will rest on him; but if not, your peace

will return to you. ⁷ Remain in the same house, eat and drink what comes from them. The laborer deserves his pay. Do not go from house to house. ⁸ And when you enter a city and they receive you, eat what is set before you, ⁹ and cure the sick in the city, saying to them, 'The kingdom of God is near.' ¹⁰ But when you go into a city and they do not receive you, then go into their squares and speak, ¹¹ 'Even the dust of your town that clings to our feet, we shake off for you. Yet know this: The kingdom of God is near.' ¹² But I say to you that it will be more sufferable in the kingdom of God for the Sodomites than for that town.

¹³ "Woe to you, Chorazin and Bethsaida. For if the mighty works were done in Tyre and Sidon that have been done with you, they would have converted long ago, sitting in sackcloth and ashes. ¹⁴ But for Tyre and Sidon it will be more sufferable than for you. ¹⁵ And you, Capharnaum, will you be exalted to heaven? You will descent even to Hades.

¹⁶ "Whoever hears you, hears me, and whoever rejects you, rejects me. But whoever hears me, hears the one who has sent me."

*10,17–24: The Return of the Seventy–Two. Jesus Giving Thanks

¹⁷ But the Seventy-Two returned filled with joy, saying, "Lord, even the demons submit to us through your name." ¹⁸ But he said to them, "I have seen Satan fall from heaven like a flash of lightning. ¹⁹ See, I have given you authority over snakes and scorpions to crush them and over each power of the enemy, and nothing will do you harm. ²⁰ But

do not rejoice that the demons submit to you; rejoice that your names are written down in heaven."

²¹ *During that time* he exulted about the spirit and said, "I thank you, Lord of heaven, for you have hidden these things from the wise and prudent and revealed them to the babes. Yes, Father, for so it has pleased you. ²² All things have been handed over to me by the Father. No one knows the Father except the Son. And someone does not recognize the Son except the Father and to whom the Son reveals it." ²³ And turning to the disciples, he said, "Blessed are the eyes that see what you see. ²⁴ For I say to you: Prophets have not seen what you see."

*10,25–28: The Question about the Conditions of Life

¹⁰,²⁵ See, a lawyer stood up; he tested him, saying, "What must I do to inherit life?" ²⁶ But he answered, saying, ²⁷ "You shall love the Lord, your God, with all your heart and with all your life and with all your strength." ²⁸ But he said to him, "You have spoken correctly."

*10,38–42: Mary and Martha

¹⁰,³⁸ But it happened on his travels that he entered a certain village. A woman named Martha received him. ³⁹ And she had a sister named Mary; she settled at the feet of Jesus and listened to his speech. ⁴⁰ But Martha was quite distracted by the elaborate serving. But she drew near, saying, "Lord, are you not bothered that my sister leaves me alone when serving? Tell her to help me." ⁴¹ But Jesus answered,

saying to her, "Martha, Martha, ⁴² Mary has chosen the good part that will not be taken away from her."

*11,1–4: The Lord's Prayer

^{11,1} And it happened as he was praying at a certain place. And after he finished, one of his disciples said to him, "Lord, teach us pray as John also has taught his disciples." ² But he said, "When you pray, do not stammer like the others. For some think that they shall be heard if they talk a lot. Instead, when you pray, say:

'Father,

{*Your* holy Spirit come *upon us and cleanse us.*}

³ Give us today your heavenly bread.

⁴ And forgive us *our* debts, as we forgive our debtors.

And lead us not into temptation.'"

*11,5–13: Instruction about Praying

^{11,5} And he said to them, "If one of you had a friend and went to him at midnight and said to him, 'Friend, lend me three loaves of bread, ⁶ for my friend from the country has arrived, and I have nothing I could set before him,' ⁷ and he would answer from inside, saying 'Do not bother me. The door is already locked, and my children are with me in bed; I cannot get up to give you something.' ⁸ {But when he keeps knocking relentlessly, -} I say to you: He will not get up and give him something because he is his friend, but because of his impertinence he will get up and give him as much as he needs. ⁹ And I say to you: Ask, then it will be given (to you). *Seek, then you will find.* Knock, then it will be

opened for you. [10] For everyone who asks, receives, and for him who knocks, it will be opened.

[11] "If the son of one of you asks for bread, will he possibly give him a stone? Or if he asks for a fish, will he possibly give him a snake? [12] Or else he asks for an egg, will he possibly give him a scorpion? [13] If even you, who are evil indeed, know how to give good gifts to your children, how much more will the heavenly Father give good gifts to those who ask him for them?"

*11,14–29: Exorcizing a Mute Demon. The Beelzebul Accusation. The Return of the Demons. Blessing Those Who Hear the Word of God. The Refusal of a Sign

[11,14] And while he was saying this, a mute possessed by a demon was brought to him; and when he cast him out, all were amazed. [15] But some of them said, "By Beelzebul, the ruler of demons, he casts out demons." But he answered, saying, "How can Satan cast out Satan?"

[16] Others tested him and demanded from him a sign from heaven. [17] But knowing their thoughts, he said to them, "Every kingdom divided against itself becomes a desert, and house after house falls down. [18] But if Satan is divided against himself, his kingdom will not last. For you say that I cast out the demons by Beelzebul. [19] If I cast out the demons by Beelzebul, by whom then do your sons cast them out? That is why they will be your judges. [20] But if I cast out the demons by the finger of God, then the kingdom of God has come to you. [21] As long as an armed strong man guards his palace, his property is in peace. [22] But if a

stronger man draws near and defeats him, he takes off his armor on which he has relied and disperses the loot. [23] *Whoever is not with me is against me, and whoever does not collect with me, scatters.*

[24] "But when the unclean spirit has gone out of a person, wandering through waterless regions to seek a resting place, but finds none, he says, 'I will return into my house from which I have gone out.' [25] And when he comes, he finds it empty, swept, and decorated. [26] He goes there and brings along seven other spirits worse than he, and they take up residence, so that this person fares worse in the end than in the beginning."

[27] But it happened, as he was saying this, that a woman in the crowd raised her voice, saying to him, "Blessed is the womb that bore you and the breasts that nursed you!" [28] But he said, "Rather, blessed are those who hear the word of God and keep it!"

[29] When the crowd gathered with him, he began to speak, "This generation is an evil generation. It demands a sign, but a sign will be given to it."

*11,33–35: The Eye as the Beacon of the Body

[11,33] "No one who lights a lamp puts it in a hiding spot or under a bushel, but on the lampstand, so that it shines for all.

[34] "Your eye is the lamp of your body. As long as your eye is truthful, your whole body is bright. But if it is evil, your body also is dark. [35] If the light in you is dark, how great then is the darkness."

41

*11,37–54: Speech to the Pharisees: Purity. Paying the Tithe. The Murder of Prophets. Conclusion

11,37 But a Pharisee invited him to dine with him. He went inside and reclined at the table. 38 But the Pharisee became doubtful and began saying to himself, "Why did he not first wash before dinner?" 39 But Jesus said to him, "You now, you Pharisees, you hypocrites! You clean the outside of the cup and the bowl, but your inside is full of greed and wickedness. 40 You fools! Did not the one who made the inside also make the outside? 41 Give property rather than alms, and then everything is clean for you.

42 "But woe to you Pharisees, for you tithe mint, rue, and every herb, but you fail the calling and the love of God.

43 "Woe to you, you Pharisees, for you love the seat of honor in the synagogues and the greetings in the squares {and the places of honor at the banquets}.

44 "Woe to you {you scribes and Pharisees,} for you are like unmarked graves, and the people walking over them do not know it."

45 But one of the lawyers answers, saying to him, "Teacher, when you say these things, you insult us too." 46 But he said, "Woe also to you lawyers. For you load the people with unbearable burdens, but you yourselves touch (them) with not a finger.

47 "Woe to you, for you erect the tombs of the prophets, but your fathers have killed them. 48 Thus you bear witness that you do not approve of the deeds of your fathers. They have killed them, but you erect.

[52] "Woe to you lawyers, for you have hidden the key of knowledge. And you do not enter yourselves, but you have hindered those who wanted to enter."

[53/54] When he said this before all the people, the Pharisees and scribes began to act with hostility and to clash with him about many things; they sought to get hold of a cause against him, so that they would find (something) to accuse him.

*12,1–12: Warning against the Hypocrisy of the Pharisees. The Appeal of Fearless Acknowledgment.

[12,1] But when crowds gathered around him, so large that they suffocated, he began to say to his disciples, "Above all, beware of the yeast of the Pharisees, that is, the hypocrisy. [2] For nothing is secret, that will not be revealed, and nothing hidden, that will not be known. [3] Whatever you have said in secret, will be heard in the light, and that which you have whispered into the ears inside the chambers, will be announced from the rooftops.

[4] "But to you, my friends, I say: Do not fear those who kill the body, but cannot kill the soul and also have nothing they can do beyond that. [5] But I show you whom you shall fear: him who has the authority after death to cast into hell. Indeed, I say: Him you shall fear!

[8] "For I say to you: Whoever acknowledges me before men, him I will acknowledge before God. [9] But everyone who denies me before men will be denied before God. [10] And whoever says something against the Son of Man will be forgiven. But whoever says something against the Holy

Spirit will not be forgiven, neither in this world nor in that to come.

¹¹ "And when they take you *into the synagogues and before the authorities and* before the rulers, do not worry beforehand how you shall answer or what you shall say. ¹² For the Holy Spirit will teach you in that hour what you must say."

*12,13–21: Warning against Greed. The Rich Farmer

¹²,¹³ Someone in the crowd said to him, "Teacher, speak with my brother, so that he divides the inheritance with me." ¹⁴ But he said to him, "Man, who appointed me to be the judge over you?" ¹⁵ And he said to them, "Be careful and guard against all greed, for a man's life does not consist in the abundance of his possessions."

¹⁶ But he told them a parable, saying: "The land of a rich man had produced well. ¹⁷ And he thought to himself, saying, 'What shall I do, for I have nothing where I can store my harvest?' ¹⁸ And he said, 'I will do this: I will pull down my barns and will make them larger, then I will store my yield there, ¹⁹ and I will say to my soul: Soul, you have abundant goods, rejoice.' ²⁰ But God spoke to him, 'You fool! This night your soul will be claimed from you. What you have piled up – to whom will it belong?'"

*12,22–34: About Worrying. Striving for the Kingdom of God

¹²,²² But he said to his disciples, "Therefore, I say to you: Do not worry about life, what you shall eat, and not about the

body, what you shall wear. [23] For life is more than food and the body more than clothing. [24] Consider the birds in the sky, they do not sow and they do not reap and they do not store in barns, and God still feeds them. By how much more do you surpass the birds! [25] But who among you can add a single cubit to his span of life? [26] Why do you then worry about the rest? [27] Consider the lilies, how they neither weave nor spin. I say to you: Not even Solomon in all his glory was clothed like one of these.

[29] "And you, do not strive after what you shall eat or what you shall drink, *and do not worry yourselves.* [30] For the nations of this world strive after that. But your Father knows that you are in need of this. [31] Rather strive first for the kingdom of God, and *all* this will be given to you in addition. [32] Fear not, you little flock, for the Father has found his pleasure therein to give you the kingdom.

[33] "Make purses for yourselves that do not wear out, an unfailing treasure in heaven where no thief comes near and no moth destroys. [34] For where your treasure is, there your heart will be also."

*12,35–48: Instruction about Vigilance and Trustworthiness

[12,35] "Your loins shall be girded and the lamps lit, [36] and you shall be like men who are waiting for their master to return from the wedding banquet, so that they, when he comes and knocks, immediately open the door for him. [37] Blessed are those slaves whom the master finds awake when he comes. Truly, I say to you: He will gird himself and have

them lay at the table. [38] When he comes to the night watch in the evening, and finds (them) so – blessed are they. [39] But you shall know this: If the owner of the house had known at what hour the thief comes, he would not have allowed that his house is broken into. [40] You also must be ready, for the Son of Man comes at an hour when you do not expect it."

[41] But Peter said to him, "Lord, do you tell this parable to us?" [42] And he said, "Who indeed is the faithful manager, the prudent, the good, whom the master puts in charge of his slaves to give them food in due time? [43] Blessed is that slave whom his master finds so doing when he arrives. [44] Truly, I say to you: He will put him in charge of all his possessions. [45] But if that slave says in his heart, 'My master is long delayed in coming,' and begins to beat the servants and maids, to eat and drink and get drunk, [46] then the master of that slave will come on a day when he does not expect him, and at an hour he does not know, and he will cut him in pieces and give him his portion with the unfaithful. [47] But that slave who did not act according to his will, although he knew it will receive a severe beating. [48] But the one who did not know and does what deserves a beating will receive a light beating. To whom much was given, from him even more will be reclaimed; and to whom much was entrusted, even more will be demanded."

*12,49–53: Peace and Discord

[12,49] "I have come to throw fire onto the earth. [51] Do you think that I have come to throw peace across the earth? No, I say to you, but rather the sword! [52] For from now on, five

will be in one house, three in discord with two and two with three. ⁵³ The father will be in discord with the son and the son with the father, and the mother with the daughter and the daughter with the mother, and the mother-in-law with the daughter-in-law and the daughter-in-law with the mother-in-law."

*12,54–59: Judging the *kairos*. Reconciling with the Adversary

¹²,⁵⁴ But he said to the crowd, "When you see a cloud rising in the west, immediately you say, 'There comes rain', and so it happens. ⁵⁵ And when you see that the south wind is blowing, you say, 'There will be heat', and it happens. ⁵⁶ You hypocrites! You judge the appearance of the sky, but you do not judge this point in time.

⁵⁷ "But why do you not find the right judgment for your-selves? ⁵⁸ For when you go with your adversary to court, make an effort while still on the way to be released from him; else, he sues you before the judge, and the judge hands you over to the bailiff, and the bailiff throws you in prison. ⁵⁹ I say to you: You will never get out from there until you have paid even the last quadrans."

*13,10–17: Healing a Daughter of Abraham on the Sabbath

¹³,¹⁰ But he was teaching in one of the synagogues on the Sabbath. ¹¹ And see, there was a woman with a spirit that crippled her for eighteen years; she was bent over and un-able to stand fully upright. ¹² But when Jesus saw her, he

said to her, "Woman, you are set free from your infirmity." ¹³ And he laid his hands on her. And immediately she stood upright and praised God.

¹⁴ But the leader of the synagogue answered, indignant because Jesus had cured on the Sabbath, saying to the crowd, "There are six days on which work shall be done; come on those days and let yourselves be cured, but not on the Sabbath." ¹⁵ But Jesus answered him and said, "You hypocrite! Does not each of you on the Sabbath untie his ox or his donkey from the manger and lead it to the trough? ¹⁶ But this daughter of Abraham, whom Satan had bound – see: for eighteen years -, did she not have to be set free from this bondage on the Sabbath?" ¹⁷ And his opponents were put to shame, but the entire crowd was rejoicing about all the wonderful deeds they saw happening through him.

*13,18–21: The Parables of the Mustard Seed and the Yeast

¹³,¹⁸ Then he said, "Who is like the kingdom of the heavens, and to what should I compare it? ¹⁹ It is like a mustard seed that someone took and sowed in his garden. And it grew and became a tree, and the birds of the sky made nests in its branches.

²⁰ "Or who is like the kingdom of God, and to what should I compare it? ²¹ It is like the leaven that a woman took and hid in wheat flour until it was all leavened."

*13,23–28: The Narrow and the Shut Door

^{13,23} But someone said to him, "Lord, will only a few be saved?" But he answered, saying, ²⁴ "Do your utmost to enter through the narrow door, for many, I say to you, seek to enter, but they do not have the strength.

²⁵ "Then, once the owner of the house gets up and locks the door, you will begin to knock, saying, 'Lord, Lord, open to us.' And he will answer, saying, 'I do not know where you come from.' ²⁶ Then you will begin to say, 'Lord, we ate and drank before you, and you taught in our squares.' ²⁷ But he will speak, saying to you, 'I do not know you (and do not know) where you come from. Go away from me, all you evildoers!' ²⁸ Then you will see: All the righteous will enter the kingdom of God, but you will be kept outside. ↑There will be wailing and teeth grinding.↓"

*14,1–6: Healing a Man with Dropsy on a Sabbath

^{14,1} *And it happened when on the Sabbath he went to the house of a leader of the Pharisees to eat bread. And all were there to observe him.* ² And see, there was a man with dropsy before him. ³ And Jesus answered, saying to the lawyers and Pharisees, "Is it lawful to cure people on the Sabbath, or not?" ⁴ But they were silent. And he took him and healed and saved him. ⁵ And he said to them, "Who of you, whose sheep or calf falls into a well, will not immediately pull it out even on a Sabbath day?" ⁶ But they did not reply to this.

*14,7–24: Admonitions about Invitations to Meals

14,7 He told a parable to those invited because he observed how they chose the best places for themselves. He said to them. 8 "When you are invited by someone to a wedding banquet, do not lay down at the place of honor, in case someone more distinguished than you arrives, 9 and then the one who invited you comes and says to you, 'Give this person your place,' and then you will receive the lowest place with shame. 10 Instead, when you are invited, go and lay down at the lowest place, so that the one who invited you, when he comes, says to you, 'Friend, move up higher.' Then you will be honored before the others attending the meal. 11 *For everyone who exalts himself will be humbled, and who humbles himself will be exalted."*

12 But he said also to the one who had invited him, "When you give a dinner or a banquet, do not invite your friends and not your brothers and not your relatives and not neighbors and not rich people, so that they do not invite you in return, and repay you. 13 But when you give a meal, invite the poor, the crippled, the lame, and the blind. 14 Then you will be blessed because, since they have nothing to repay you, you will be repaid at the resurrection of the righteous."

15 But when one of those attending the meal heard this, he said to him, "Blessed, who takes the meal in the kingdom of God!" 16 But he said to him, "A man gave a dinner and invited many. 17 And at the hour of the dinner, he sent his slave to say to the invited, 'Come, for everything is ready now.' 18 But they all began to make excuses as if with one

voice. The first said to him, 'I have bought a field and must go out and look at it. I beg you to excuse me.' [19] And another said, 'I have bought five yoke of oxen and am setting out to inspect them; that is why I cannot come.' [20] And another said, 'I have taken a wife; that is why I cannot come.' [21] When the slave returned, he reported this to his master. Then the owner of the house became upset, saying to his slave, 'Go out quickly into the squares and streets of the town, and bring the poor, the crippled, the blind, and the lame here.' [22] And the slave said, 'What you ordered has been done, but there is still room.' [23] And the master said to his slave, 'Go out to the roads and hedges, and compel people to come in, so that my house will be filled. [24] For I say to you: None of those invited will taste my dinner.'"

*14,25–35: Requirements for Being a Disciple

[14,25] But large crowds traveled with him, and he turned to them, saying, [26] "When someone comes to me and does not hate his father and his mother and his wife and children and the brothers and sisters – and not even his own life, then he cannot be my disciple. [27] He who does not carry his cross and follow behind me cannot be my disciple.

[28] "For who of you, intending to build a tower, will not first sit down and calculate the cost, whether it suffices for completion, [29] so that, when he has laid the foundation but cannot build, not everyone who sees it, will say, [30] 'This man began to erect a building, but he cannot complete it'?

[31] "Or what king, going out to meet in battle with another king, will not sit down immediately and consult whether he

is able with ten thousand to oppose the one who marches against him with twenty thousand? [32] And when he cannot, while the other is still far away, he sends a delegation and asks for what will (lead) to peace. [33] Likewise each one of you: He who does not give up all his possessions cannot be my disciple.

[34] "Salt is good. But when even salt becomes dull, what shall be used for seasoning? [35] It is fit neither for the field nor for the manure pile; it will be thrown away and crushed by the people."

*15,3–10: The Parables of the Lost Sheep and the Lost Coin

[15,3] But he told them the following parable, saying: [4] "Which one of you, having a hundred sheep and losing one of them, does not leave behind the ninety-nine in the wilderness and walk off to seek the lost one until he finds it? [5] And when he finds it – [7] truly, I say to you: He will have more joy about it than about the ninety-nine. Likewise, there will be joy in heaven *when one of the lost is found.*

[8] "Or what woman having ten drachmas, when losing a single one, will not light a lamp and sweep the house and search carefully until she finds it? [10] Likewise, I say to you: There will be joy before the angels of God *when one of the lost is found.*"

*16,1–13: The Parable of the Dishonest Manager. Being Faithful in a Very Little and in Much

16,1 But he said to the disciples, "There was a rich man who had a manager; charges were brought to him that this man was squandering his property. 2 And he summoned him, saying to him, 'What is this that I hear about you? Give me an accounting of your management because you cannot be a manager any longer.' 3 But the manager said to himself, 'What shall I do, for my master is taking the management away from me? For hard work, I am not strong enough; to beg, I am ashamed. 4 I know what I must do, so that they will welcome me into their homes when I am dismissed from management.' 5 And he summoned each one of his master's debtors and said to the first, 'How much do you owe my master?' 6 But he answered, 'A hundred measures of oil.' But he said to him, 'Take your bill and write down fifty.' 7 Then he said to another, 'And how much do you owe?' But he replied, 'A hundred measures of wheat.' He said to him, 'Take your bill and write down eighty.'

8 "That is why I say to you: The sons of this world are cleverer in dealing with their own generation than the sons of light. 9 And I say to you: Make friends for yourselves by means of the unrighteous mammon. 10 *Whoever is dependable with the least is dependable also with much; and whoever is dishonest with the least is dishonest also with much.*

11 "If then you have not been dependable with the dishonest mammon, who shall entrust to you with the true riches? 12 And if you have not been found dependable with what belongs to a stranger, who shall give you what is

mine? [13] No slave can serve two masters. For he will either hate the one and love the other or he will be devoted to the one and despise the other. You cannot serve God and the mammon."

*16,14–18: Opposing the Pharisees: Greed. The Law and the Prophets. Divorce and Remarriage

[16,14] The Pharisees, who are lovers of money, heard this and ridiculed him. [15] And he said to them, "You are the ones portraying yourselves before the people as righteous, but God knows your hearts. For what is regarded highly by people is an abomination before God.

[16] "The law and the prophets {were prophesied} until John. Since then the kingdom of God is being proclaimed. [17] Heaven and earth passes away faster than even a single stroke of the words of the Lord. [18] "If someone dismisses the wife and marries another, he commits adultery; and if someone marries someone dismissed by a husband, then he equally commits adultery."

*16,19–31: The Parable of the Poor Lazarus and the Rich Neves

[16,19] But he also told another parable: "There was a rich man *named Neves*; he dressed in purple and byssus and enjoyed every day lavishly. [20] And a poor man named Lazarus, covered with sores, lay at his gate. [21] And he longed to satisfy his hunger with what fell from the rich man's table. But even the dogs came and licked his sores. [22] But it happened that the poor man died and was carried away by angels into

Abraham's lap. The rich man also died and was buried in Hades. ²³ He is now raising his eyes and sees, while he is in pain, Abraham far away and Lazarus rest in his lap. ²⁴ And he called out, saying, 'Father Abraham, have mercy on me and send Lazarus to dip the tip of his finger in water and cool my tongue; for I am in agony in this burning heat.' ²⁵ But Abraham said, 'Child, remember that during your lifetime you received the good things, but Lazarus equally the bad things. And now he is being comforted here, but you are in agony. ²⁶ Besides, between you and us there is a deep abyss, so that those who might want to pass from here to you cannot do so, and they also cannot come across from there to us.' ²⁷ 'Then I beg you, father, that you send him to my father's house, ²⁸ for I have five brothers, that he warns them, so that they will not also come to this place of torment.' ²⁹ But he says to him, 'They have Moses and the prophets {there}; to them they should listen.' ³⁰ But he said, 'No, father; rather, if someone goes to them from the dead, they will turn back.' ³¹ But he said, 'If they have not listened to Moses and the prophets, they would, if one of the dead came {to them}, also not listen to him.'"

*17,1–10: Speech to the Disciples about Temptation and about the Power of Faith

¹⁷,¹ But he said to his disciples, "It is impossible that no offence comes. But woe to {him} by whom {the offence} comes! ² It would be better for him {if he were never born or} if a millstone was hung around his neck and he was thrown into the sea than that he causes one of these little

ones to fall. ³ Guard yourselves! If your brother sins against you, set him straight. And if he repents, forgive him. ⁴ And if he sins against you seven times in one day and turns to you seven times and says, 'I repent,' you shall forgive him."

⁵ The apostles said to him, "Give us more faith." ⁶ But he said to them, "If you had faith like a mustard seed, you could {say to this mountain, 'Go from here to over there,' and it would go over there; and you could} say to a fig tree, 'Transplant yourself,' and it would obey you.

⁷ "Who among you, having a slave for plowing or for grazing, will say to him when he comes from the field, 'Come, lay down at once'? ⁸ He will rather say to him, 'Prepare something to eat for me, and then gird yourself and serve me until I have eaten and drunk; and after that you may eat and drink.' ⁹ Will he thank the slave that he has done what was commanded {to him}? {I think not.} ¹⁰ So also you, when that is being done whatever I ordered.'"

*17,11–18: Cleansing Ten Lepers

^{17,11} And it happened on the way to Jerusalem that he passed through the midst of Samaria and Galilee and Jericho. ¹² And as he entered a certain village where they were at the time, see, ten lepers stood at a distance, ¹³ and they cried out with a loud voice, "Jesus, Master, have mercy on us!" ¹⁴ And when he saw them, he said to them, "You are healed. Go and show yourselves to the priests." And it happened as they went that they were made clean.

¹⁵ And when one of them saw that he was cleansed, he turned back and praised God with a loud voice, ¹⁶ and he fell

down on his face at his feet and thanked him. But he was a Samaritan. [17] But Jesus answered, saying, "These ten were made clean. Where are the nine others? [18] Cannot one of them be found who returns and wants to give the honor to God except this foreigner? {↑[4,27] There were many lepers in the days of the prophet Elisha, but no one was cleansed except Naaman the Syrian↓}." [19] And he said to him, "Get up and go. Your faith has saved you."

*17,20f: About the Coming of the Kingdom of God

[17,20] But when he was asked by the Pharisees when the kingdom of God was coming, he answered to them, saying, "The kingdom of God is not coming with (the possibility of) observation, [21] nor can they say, 'Look, here, look there!' See, the kingdom of God is in your midst."

*17,22–37: About the Coming of the Son of Man

[17,22] But he said to the disciples, "Days will come when you will long to see just one of the days of the Son of Man, but you will see nothing. [23] And they will say to you, 'Look here! Look there!' Do not go there and do not follow (them).' [24] For just as the lightning bolt gleams when it flashes from the sky, so will also the coming of the Son of Man be. [25] But first it is necessary that he suffers many things and is rejected by this generation.

[26] "Just as it happened in the days of Noah, so will it be in the days of the Son of Man: [27] they ate, they drank, they married, they were given in marriage – until the day Noah entered the ark; then the flood came and destroyed them

all. [28] Similar to what happened in the days of Lot: they ate, they drank, they traded, they sold, they planted, they built; [29] on the day that Lot left Sodom, it rained fire from heaven and destroyed them all.

[30] "So will it also be on the day of the Son of Man on which he is revealed. [31] Whoever is on the housetop at that hour, but has his belongings in the house, shall not come down to get them, and similarly, shall not look back who is on the field. [32] Remember Lot's wife. [33] Whoever seeks to save his life, will lose it; but whoever loses it, will save it.

[34] "I say to you: In that night there will be two in one bed, one will be taken, the other will be left. [35] Two will grind at the same mill, one will be taken, the other will be left. [36] Two on a field, one will be taken, the other will be saved."

[37] They answered, saying to him, "Where, Lord?" But he said to them, "Where the corpse is, there gather also the eagles."

*18,1–8: Parable of the Pleading Widow

[18,1] He told them a parable about the need always to pray and not to let up: [2] "There was a judge in the city who had no fear of God and showed no consideration for people. [3] But in that city was also a widow who came to him, saying, 'Grant me justice against my opponent.' [4] And for a long time he was not inclined. But after that he came to his senses, saying, 'Though I have no fear of God and show no consideration for people, [5] I will, since this widow troubles me, grant her justice, so that she may not come at last and slap me in the face.'" [6] But Jesus answered, saying, "Listen

to what the unjust judge says. [7] And will not God grant justice to his chosen who cry out to him day and night? And will he hesitate with them? [8] I say to you: He will grant justice to them shortly. But when the Son of Man comes, will he find faith on earth?"

*18,9–14: The Parable of the Pharisee and Tax Collector in the Temple

[18,9] He also spoke to some who feel self-assured about being righteous, and who look down on others: [10] "Two men went up to the temple to pray, one a Pharisee, one a tax collector. [11] The Pharisee stood by himself and prayed thus, 'God, I thank you that I am not like the other people – thieves, crooks, adulterers, or even like this tax collector. [12] I fast twice a week; I give a tenth of everything I buy.' [13] But the tax collector stood far off and did not even want to lift his eyes to heaven; instead, he beat his breast, saying, 'God, be merciful to me, a sinner!' [14] I say to you: This man went back down to his home justified, more than that Pharisee did. *For everyone who exalts himself will be humbled, but everyone who humbles himself will be exalted.*"

*18,15–17: Blessing of the Children

[18,15] They brought children to him, so that he might touch them. *But when they saw it,* the disciples threatened them. [16] But Jesus called for them, saying, "Let the children come to me for to them belongs the kingdom of the heavens. [17] Truly, I say to you: If one does not accept the kingdom of the heavens like a child, he will not enter into it."

*18,18–23: The Question about the Requirements for Eternal Life

18,18 Someone asked him, saying, "Good Teacher, what must I do to inherit eternal life?" 19 But he replied, "Do not call me good. (Only) one is good, {the Father}. 20 *But he said*, "I know the commandments: 'You shall not murder. You shall not commit adultery. You shall not steal. You shall not bear false witness. Honor your father and mother. 21 I have observed all these since my youth." 22 But when Jesus heard this, he said to him, "You lack one thing: Sell all that you own, and give it to the poor, then you will have a treasure in heaven. And after that: come, and follow me." 23 But when he heard this, he became sad because he was very rich.

*18,24–30: Wealth and Succession

18,24 But when Jesus saw him, he said, "How difficult it is for the wealthy to enter into the kingdom of God."

26 But the listeners said, "Who then can be saved?" 27 But he said, "What is impossible for men is possible for God." 28 But Peter said, "See, we have left the possessions and have followed you." 29 But he said to them, "Truly, I say to you: There is nobody who has left house or parents or brothers or sisters or wife or children for the sake of the kingdom of God 30 who does not receive seventyfold in this time, and eternal life in the world to come."

*18,35–43: Healing a Blind Man in Jericho

^{18,35} But it happened as he approached Jericho that a blind man was sitting by the roadside begging. ³⁶ But when he heard the crowd going by, he asked what this could be. ³⁷ And he was told, "Jesus is passing by." ³⁸ And he shouted, "Jesus, Son of David, have mercy on me!" ⁴⁰ But he stood still and asked to have the man brought to him. But when he came near, he asked him, ⁴¹ "What do you want me to do for you?" But he said, "Lord, that I can see again." ⁴² And Jesus {answered and} said to him, "You shall see again. Your faith has saved you." ⁴³ And immediately he could see again, and all the people, who had observed it, praised God.

*19,1–10: The Conversion of Zacchaeus

^{19,1} And after he had entered, he passed through Jericho. ² And see, there was a man named Zacchaeus, a rich chief tax collector. ³ And he sought to see Jesus, who he was, but he could not because of the crowd for he was short in stature. ⁴ And he ran ahead and climbed a fig tree to see him, since he was going to pass that (way). ⁵ And it happened as he passed by that he saw him, saying to him, "Zacchaeus, hurry, come down. For today I must stay at your house." ⁶ And he hurried down and welcomed him with joy. ⁸ But Zacchaeus stood there and said to Jesus, "See, Lord, half of my possessions I give to the poor, and if I have defrauded anyone of anything, I pay it back fourfold." ⁹ But Jesus said to him, "Today salvation has come to this house. ¹⁰ For the Son of Man came to save that which is lost."

*19,11–28: The Parable of the Ten Pounds. Entry into Jerusalem

^{19,11} But when they heard this, he told them yet another parable: ¹² "A nobleman went to a distant country. ¹³ He summoned his ten slaves and gave them ten pounds, saying to them, 'Do business while I am underway.' ¹⁵ And it happened when he returned, that he summoned the ten slaves to whom he had given the silver to find out what they had gained. ¹⁶ But the first came forward, saying, 'Lord, your pound has earned ten additional pounds.' ¹⁷ And he said to him, 'Well done, good slave, for you were trustworthy with the least.' ¹⁸ And the second came, saying, 'Lord, your pound has yielded five pounds.' ²⁰ And the other came, saying, 'Lord, see, (here is) your pound which I had kept safe wrapped in a piece of cloth. ²¹ For I was afraid of you because you are a harsh man; you take what you did not deposit, and you reap what you did not sow.' ²² He said to him, 'I will judge you by your own words, wicked slave. You knew that I am a harsh man, that I take what I did not deposit and reap what I did not sow. ²³ And why did you not put my silver into the bank? Then I could have collected it with interest at my arrival.' ²⁴ And to the bystanders he said, 'Take the pound from him and give it to the one who has ten pounds.' ²⁶ 'I say to you: Everyone who has will be given; from him who has nothing, even that will be taken away what he deems to have. ²⁷ {And throw the useless slave into the outer darkness. There will be wailing and teeth grinding'}."

²⁸ And after he had told this, he went on ahead *ascending* to Jerusalem.

*19,36–40: The Acclamation at the Mount of Olives

19,36 But when he walked along, they kept spreading their cloaks on the road. 37 As he was approaching the path descending from the Mount of Olives, the whole multitude of his disciples began to praise God joyfully with a loud voice for all the deeds of power that they had seen. 38 They said, "{Blessed be the king!} Peace in heaven and glory in the highest!" 39 And some of the Pharisees in the crowd said to him, "Teacher, reprimand your disciples." 40 And he answered, saying, "I say to you: If they keep silent, the stones will cry out."

*20,1–8: Questioning Jesus' Authority. The Intent to Arrest Jesus

20,1 And it happened, as he was teaching the people in the temple on one of the days, that the Pharisees got up 2 and spoke, saying to him, "Explain to us, by what authority are you doing these things, and who has given you this authority!" 3 But he answered, saying to them, "I will also ask you a question which you shall answer me: 4 Was the baptism of John from heaven or of men?" 5 But they deliberated and said to one another, "If we say, 'from heaven,' he will say, 'Why then did you not believe him?' 6 But if we say, 'of men,' all of the people will stone us because they are convinced that John is a prophet." 7 And they answered that they knew not from where it came. 8 And Jesus said to them, "Neither will I tell you by what authority I am doing these things."

¹⁹ And they sought to lay hands on him, but they were afraid.

*20,20–26: The Question about Paying Taxes to the Emperor

^{20,20} And they left, sending spies *who pretended to be honest* to trap him by way of his speech, so that they could extradite him to the governor. ²¹ And they asked him, saying, "Teacher, we know that you speak and teach righteously, that you show deference to no one, but teach the way of God in accordance with the truth. ²² Are we permitted to pay taxes to the emperor, or not?" ²³ But he perceived their wickedness, saying to them, ²⁴ "Show me a *denarius*. Whose image and inscription does it bear?" They answered, saying, "That of the emperor." ²⁵ But he said to them, "Give to the emperor what is the emperor's and to God what is God's." ²⁶ And they were not able in the presence of the people to trap him by a word, and they marveled at his answer and were silent.

*20,27–40: The Question about the Resurrection

^{20,27} But some of the Sadducees came who denied that there was any resurrection. They asked him, ²⁸ saying, "Teacher, Moses wrote down for us: If someone's brother dies childless but has a wife, then his brother shall take the wife and rouse descendants for his brother. ²⁹ With us were seven brothers. The first took a wife but died childless. ³⁰ Also the second ³¹ and the third. And in the same way all seven died childless. ³² Finally the woman also died. ³³ Now, in the

resurrection, whose wife will she be? For seven men had her as wife." ³⁴ And Jesus said to them, "The sons of this age are being conceived and they conceive. ³⁵ But those whom God has considered worthy of inheriting that age and of the resurrection from the dead, they do not marry and are not given in marriage. ³⁶ For they will no longer die because they are like the angels of God and were made sons of the resurrection."

³⁹ But some of the scribes answered, saying, "Teacher, you have spoken well." ⁴⁰ For they no longer dared to ask him anything.

*20,41–44: The Messiah is David's Lord, Not His Son

²⁰,⁴¹ But he said to the scribes, "What do you think about the Christ: Whose son is he?" They said to him, "David's." ⁴² He said to them, "How then can David in the *holy* spirit call him his Lord when he says, 'The Lord says to my Lord, Sit at my right hand ⁴³ until I have laid your enemies under your feet'? ⁴⁴ David thus calls him his Lord, so how can he be his son?"

*20,45–47: Warning about the Scribes

²⁰,⁴⁵ *But while all the people listened, he said to his disciples,* ⁴⁶ "Beware of the scribes who like to walk around in long robes and love the greetings in the marketplace and the prominent seat in the synagogues and places of honor at banquets. ⁴⁷ They devour the houses of widows while saying long prayers in pretense. They will receive a harsher judgment."

*21,1–4: The Widow's Offering

21,1 But when he looked up, he saw the rich putting their gifts into the treasury. 2 But he also saw a poor widow who deposited two lepta there, which is one quadrans. 3 And he said: "Truly, I say to you: This widow, who is poor, has put in more than all (the others). 4 For all of them have put down (something) out of their abundance toward the gifts for God, but she, out of her privation, has put in her entire livelihood that she owned."

*21,5–36: Speech about the End Times

21,5 And when some were saying about the temple that it was adorned with beautiful stones and consecrated gifts, he said, 6 "Look at that. Days will come when {in this wall} no stone will be left upon another that will not have been broken out."

7 {The disciples} asked him, saying, "Teacher, when will this be? And what is the sign of his coming?" 8 But he said, "Beware that you will not be led astray. Many will come in my name and say, 'I am {the Christ', and they will lead many astray}, or, 'The time is near'; do not run after them. 9 But when you will hear of wars and insurrections, do not be afraid. For all this must take place first, but the end will not follow immediately. 10 Kingdom will rise against kingdom and nation against nation, 11 and there will be ↑plagues and famines↓ and earthquakes; from the sky frightful portents will *appear* and blizzards will *flare up*.

12 "But before all this occurs, they will lay their hands on you and persecute you, they will hand you over to

synagogues and prisons, before kings and governors, for the sake of my name. ¹³ This will endow you with a testimony {as well as salvation}. ¹⁴ Therefore, settle it in your hearts that you not prepare in advance, what must be brought to your defense. ¹⁵ I will provide you myself with voice and wisdom all your adversaries will not be able to withstand or contradict. ¹⁶ But you will be handed over even by parents and brothers and relatives and friends, and they will put (some) of you to death. ¹⁷ And you will be hated by all for the sake of my name. ¹⁹ But through being steadfast, you will save yourselves.

²⁰ "When you see Jerusalem surrounded by armies, then you will know that its desolation is near. ²³ Woe to the pregnant and nursing in those days! For there will be great distress in the land and wrath against this people. ²⁴ And they will fall by the edge of the sword and be taken away as captives to all pagan nations, and Jerusalem will be crushed by the Gentiles.

²⁵ "And there will be signs in the sun, moon, and stars, and on the earth, anxiety among the nations and hopelessness before the roaring of the sea and the waves, ²⁶ when men will faint from fear and expectation of what is coming over the earth; for even the powers in heaven will be shaken. ²⁷ And then they will see the Son of Man coming from heaven with great power. ²⁸ But when this will happen, you will stand up and raise your heads, for your redemption has come near."

²⁹ And he told them a parable: "Look at the fig tree and at every tree. ³⁰ When they sprout fruit, people know that summer is near. ³¹ And you likewise; when you see all this

happening, you know that the kingdom of God is near. [32] Truly, I say to you, This heaven and the earth will not pass unless all this is completed. [33] Heaven and earth will pass away, but the words of the Lord will not pass away.

[34] "Guard yourselves that your hearts will not become heavy with overindulgence and drunkenness and everyday worries, and that this sudden day will not surprise you [35] like a snare. For it will fall upon all who live on the face of the whole earth. [36] But at every hour be alert and pray that you are deemed worthy of escaping all these happenings to come, and that you will stand before the Son of Man."

*21,37f: Concluding Summary: Teaching in Jerusalem

[21,37] But he spent the day teaching in the temple, staying overnight on the Mount of Olives. [38] And all the people came to him early in the morning to hear him in the temple.

*22,1–6: The Intent to Kill Jesus by the Chief Priests. The Betrayal of Judas

[22,1] But the feast of unleavened bread, which is called the Passover, was near. [2] And the chief priests and the scribes looked (for an opportunity) of how to destroy him, for they were afraid of the people. [4] But Judas, *who is called the Iscariot and came from the group of the Twelve*, went away and conferred with the chief priests about how he might extradite him. [5] And they promised to give him money. [6] And he looked for a favorable opportunity to extradite him.

*22,7–13: The Preparation of the Passover Meal

22,7 But the day of Passover came on which the Passover lamb had to be slaughtered. 8 And he sent *two of his disciples*, saying, "Go and make preparations, so that we (can) eat the Passover lamb." 9 But they said to him, "Where do you want us to make preparations for eating the Passover lamb?" 10 But he said to them, "See, when you enter the city, you will be met by a man carrying an earthen jar of water. Follow him into the house he enters. 11 And say to the owner of the house, 'The teacher says, Where is the room in which I may eat the Passover lamb with my disciples?' 12 And he will show you a large room upstairs furnished with cushions. Make the preparations there." 13 But they went and found everything as he had told them, and they made ready the Passover.

*22,14–23: The Last Supper. Announcing the Betrayal

22,14 And he took his place, and the {twelve} apostles with him. 15 And he said, "I have eagerly desired to eat the Passover meal with you before my suffering." 17 And he took a cup, gave thanks, saying, "Take this, and divide it among yourselves. 18 For I say to you: From now on I will not drink of the fruit of the vine until the kingdom of God comes." 19 And he took a loaf of bread, blessed it, and gave it to the disciples, saying, "This is my body. 21 But see, the hand of him who surrenders me is with me on the table. 22 While the Son of Man follows his calling, woe to him by whom the Son of Man is extradited!" 23 Then they began to deliberate with one another which one of them would do this.

*22,24–34: Meal Conversations: The Disciples Disputing Status. The Announcement of Peter' Denial

22,24 But a dispute arose among them as to who was the greatest. 25 But he said to them, "The kings of nations rule over them; and those exerting authority over them are called benefactors. 26 But not so with you. Indeed, the greatest among you shall be like the smallest, and the leader shall be rather like the servant than the one 27 who lies at the table. For, I came into your midst not as one who lies at the table, but as a servant. 28 But you, who have stayed with me in my trials, have grown in my service like a servant. 29 And I assign the kingdom to you, as my Father has assigned it to me, 30 so that you will eat and drink at my table in my kingdom, and you will sit on twelve thrones judging the twelve tribes of Israel."

31 But he said to Simon, "Simon, see, Satan has petitioned to sift you like wheat." 33 But he said to him, "Lord, I am ready to go with you even to prison and into death!" 34 But he said, "I say to you: The cock will not crow today until you have denied me for three times that you do not know me."

*22,39–46: Prayer on the Mount of Olives

22,39 And he went out and walked, as was his custom, to the Mount of Olives. But the disciples followed him. 40 But when he reached the place, he said to them, "Pray that you are not going to be tested." 41 And he withdrew about a stone's throw from them, fell on his knees, and prayed, 42 saying,

"Father, not my will but yours be done. If you are willing, remove this cup from me."

⁴⁵ And he got up from prayer, went to the disciples, and found them sleeping of grief. ⁴⁶ And he said to them, "You sleep? Get up and pray, so that you are not going to be tested."

*22,47–53: Encounter with the Arrest Squad

^{22,47} While he was still speaking, see, there was a large crowd, and the one called Judas Iscariot, one of the Twelve, led them. And Judas came near to kiss him. For he had given them this sign, whom I will kiss, that is he. ⁴⁸ And he said to Judas, "With a kiss you extradite the Son of Man?"

⁵² *But Jesus answered and said to them,* "As if apprehending a robber, you have moved out with swords and clubs? ⁵³ I was with you daily in the temple, but you did not lift your hands against me. But this is your hour and the power of darkness!"

*22,54–65: Peter's Denial. The Mockery of Jesus by the Guards

^{22,54} But they seized him and led him into the house of the high priest. But Peter followed him at a distance. ⁵⁵ And when they had kindled a fire in the middle of the courtyard and sat down together, Peter also sat down among them to warm himself. ⁵⁶ But when a servant-girl saw him sitting in the firelight, she looked at him closely, saying, "This man also was with him." ⁵⁷ But he denied it, saying, "I do not know him." ⁵⁸ And when a short while later someone else

saw him, he told the same. But Peter said, "Man, it is not me." [59] And about an hour later, another one declared, "I tell the truth, this man was with him, for he is a Galilean." [60] But Peter said, "Man, I do not know what you are talking about!" And immediately, while he was still speaking, a cock crowed. [61] And Jesus turned and looked at Peter. And he remembered the word of Jesus, how he had said to him, "Before the cock crows, you will have betrayed me for three times that you do not know me."

[63] And the men who guarded (him) mocked him, clubbed [64] and beat him, saying, "Prophesy! Who is it that struck you?" [65] And they voiced many other insults against him.

*22,66–71: The Interrogation before the High Council

[22,66] And when day came, the elders of the people and the chief priests and the scribes assembled, and they brought him before their council, [67] saying, "Are you the Christ?" But he said, "If I tell you, you will not believe it. [69] From now on the Son of Man will be seated at the right hand of the power of God." [70] Then they all said, "Are you then the Son of God?" But he said to them, "You say it." [71] But they said, "What further witness do we need? For, we have heard it ourselves from his own mouth."

*23,1–5: The Trial of Jesus I: Transfer to Pilate. Interrogation and First Judgment by Pilate

[23,1] And they rose and led him to Pilate. [2] They began to accuse him, saying, "We have found that this man incites the people {and dissolves the law and the prophets,} and orders

to pay no taxes {and turns away the wives and children *from us because they are not baptized like we are and not cleansed*;} and says that he was himself the Christ, a king." [3] But Pilate asked him, saying, "Are you the Christ?" And he answered, saying, "You say it." [4] But Pilate said to the chief priests and to the crowd, "I find no guilt with this man." [5] But they were insistent, saying, "He stirs up the people throughout Judea, beginning from Galilee all the way here."

*23,6–12: The Trial of Jesus II: Transfer to Herod. Interrogation. Mockery

[23,6] But when Pilate heard this, he asked whether the man was from Galilee. [7] And when he learned that he was under Herod's domain, he sent him to Herod who was himself in Jerusalem in these days. [8] And when Herod saw Jesus, he was very glad. [9] He questioned him. But he did not answer him. [10] But the chief priests and the scribes stood by and accused him most vehemently. [11] And even Herod, together with his soldiers, treated him with contempt and mocked him. He put on him a lustrous robe and sent him back to Pilate. [12] But Pilate and Herod, who had been in discord, became friends on that day.

*23,13–25: The Trial of Jesus III: Repeating the Innocence Declaration. Barabbas. Sentencing

[23,13] But Pilate called together the chief priests and the leaders and the people, [14] saying to them, "You have presented to me this man for inciting the people, and see, as I have interrogated him in your presence, I have found no guilt

with this man, ¹⁵ and neither has Herod, for he sent him back to us. And see, there is nothing he has done to deserve death. ¹⁶ I will, therefore, (have him) chastised and then released."

¹⁸ But they all shouted out together, saying, "Keep this man here, but release Barrabas for us!" ¹⁹ He had been thrown into prison *for an insurrection that had occurred in the city, and* for murder. ↑{¹⁷ But he was obliged during the feast to release someone for them.}↓ ²⁰ But again, Pilate addressed them because he wanted to release Jesus. ²¹ But they shouted, saying, "Crucify, crucify him!" ²² But he spoke for the third time, "What evil has he done? I have found on him nothing at all to deserve death. I will, therefore, chastise and release him." ²³ But they kept charging with a loud voice and demanded to crucify him; and their shouting grew louder.

²⁴ Then Pilate made the judgment that their demand shall be granted. ²⁵ But he released the man they wanted, the one thrown into prison for murder; Jesus, however, he surrendered to their will.

*23,26–32: The Way of the Cross: Simon of Cyrene. The Women of Jerusalem. Two Criminals

²³,²⁶ And when they led him away, they seized one Simon, a Cyrenian, who came from the field. And on him they laid the cross to carry it behind Jesus.

²⁷ But a great number of people and women followed him who wailed and grieved for him. ²⁸ But Jesus turned to them, saying, "Daughters of Jerusalem, do not weep for me

{and do not lament}. But weep for yourselves and for your children, ²⁹ for days will come when they say, 'Blessed are the barren and the wombs that have not born and the breasts that have not nursed.' ³⁰ Then they will begin to say to the mountains, 'Fall on us', and to the hills, 'Cover us.' ³¹ For if they do this with fresh wood, what will happen with the dry?"

³² But they also led two malefactors with him to the execution, *Joathas and Maggathras*.

*23,33–49: Crucifixion and Death of Jesus

^{23,33} And when they came to the place that is called The Skull, they crucified him and at the same time also the malefactors, one to his right hand, the other to his left.

³⁵ And the people stood by and stared. But they derided him and said to him, "You have saved others. Save yourself if you are the Son of God, if you are the Christ!" ³⁶ But the soldiers also mocked him; they came near and offered him sour wine, ³⁷ saying, "Hail, King of the Jews!", {and they placed a crown of thorns on him.} ³⁸ But there was an inscription with him, "The King of the Jews." ³⁹ But one of the malefactors blasphemed him. ⁴⁰ But the other answered, threatened him, and said, "Do you fear not even God? Do we not stand under the same judgment? ⁴¹ We, indeed, justly; for we get what our deeds deserve. But this man has done nothing evil." ⁴² And he said, "Jesus, remember me when you come into your kingdom."

⁴⁴ And it was already at the sixth hour, and darkness came over the whole earth until the ninth hour, ⁴⁵ and the

sun became dark. [46] Jesus cried out with a loud voice and died; {and the curtain of the temple tore.}

[47] And the centurion called out and praised God, saying, "Truly, this man was righteous." [48] And the crowds of people, who had gathered for this spectacle, saw what happened. They beat their breasts and foreheads and returned, {saying, "Woe to us, this happened today because of our sins. For the destruction of Jerusalem has come near."} [49] But all who knew him, remained standing. The women, who had followed him from Galilee, also saw it.

*23,50–56: The Burial of Jesus

[23,50] And see, a man named Joseph [53] took {the body} down, wrapped it in a linen cloth, and laid it in a rock-hewn tomb.

[54] That was on the day before the Sabbath. [55] But two women, who had come with him from Galilee, followed. They saw his tomb. [56] And the women returned and kept the rest on the Sabbath.

*24,1–11: Finding the Empty Tomb. The Angels' Proclamation. Message to the Disciples

[24,1] And on the first day of the week they came at early dawn to the tomb and brought what they had prepared. {They thought among themselves, "Who will roll away the stone indeed?"} [2] But when they arrived, they found the stone rolled away. [3] But when they went inside, they did not find the body. [4] And while they were confused about him, it happened: See, two men in dazzling clothes approached them. [5] But when they became fearful and bowed their faces to

the ground, they said to them, "Why do you look for him who is alive among the dead? ⁶ Remember what he said to you when he was still with you: ⁷ That it is necessary that the Son of Man be extradited." ⁸ *And they remembered his words.*

⁹ And they returned from the tomb and told all this to the {apostles} and to all the others, ¹⁰ Mary Magdalene and Joanna and Mary (the wife) of James. ¹¹ But these words seemed to them like idle talk, and they did not believe them.

*24,13–35: Appearance to Emmaus/Amaus and Cleopas

²⁴,¹³ Two of them, named Emmaus {and Cleopas}, were on their way to a village about 60 stadia from Jerusalem. ¹⁴ But they talked with each other about all these events. ¹⁵ And it happened, while they were talking, that Jesus came near and went with them. ¹⁶ But their eyes were held, so that they did not recognize him. ¹⁷ But he said, "What are these words you exchange in sadness when walking?" ¹⁸ But one of two named Cleopas answered, saying to him, "Are you the only visitor in Jerusalem who does not know what has happened in the city in these days?" ¹⁹ But he said to him, "What happened?" "The things concerning Jesus the Nazorean: he was a prophet, mighty in word and deed before God and all the people, ²⁰ how the chief priests and leaders extradited him to be sentenced to death, and how they crucified him. ²¹ And we had the hope that he is the one who has come to redeem Israel. But this is now the third day since this happened. ²² But a few women have also bewildered us. They

came to the tomb very early in the morning, ²³ and when they did not find his body, they came back, saying that they had seen an apparition of angels who said that he was alive."

²⁵ Then he said to them, "You are without understanding and too unwieldy to believe everything I have said to you. ²⁶ For it was necessary that the Christ suffers all this." ²⁸ And they came near the village to which they were going, and he acted as if he wanted to go on. ²⁹ But they urged him, saying, "Stay with us, because the day has turned to evening." And he went inside to stay with them. ³⁰ And it happened when he lay down that he took bread, spoke the blessing, and gave it to them. ³¹ But when they received the bread from him, their eyes opened and they recognized him. But he became invisible before them. ³² Then they said to each other, "Was not our heart under a veil when he talked to us on the road?"

³³ And saddened they got up *at that hour* and returned to Jerusalem; they found the apostles gathered and said that Jesus has been made known when breaking the bread.

*24,36–43: Jesus' Appearance to the Disciples

²⁴,³⁶ And while they were still talking about this, he himself stood in their midst. ³⁷ But being scared and becoming fearful, they believed to see a ghost. ³⁸ And he said to them, "Why were you scared? ³⁹ Look at my hands and my feet, for a ghost has no bones as you see I have." ⁴¹ But when they were still disbelieving, he said to them, "Have you something here to eat?" ⁴² But they gave him a piece of

roasted fish. [43] And he took it and ate it before their eyes. {And the rest he gave to them.}

*24,50–53: Commissioning of the Disciples. The Departure of Jesus. The Return to Jerusalem

[50] But he led them out to Bethany. And lifting up his hands he blessed them. {And he sent out the apostles to proclaim to all the Gentile nations.} [51] And it happened when he blessed them that he departed from them. [52] And they returned to Jerusalem full of joy. [53] And they praised God at all times.

Notes

Notes

Printed in Great Britain
by Amazon

44083115R00050